SCARBOROUGH TRAMWAYS

including the Scarborough Cliff Lifts

Barry M Marsden

Series editor Robert J.Harley

MP Middleton Press

Front cover picture see caption no. 67

Back cover pictures: top - see caption no. 28
                            lower - see caption no. 93

Cover colours: these reflect the dark red and cream livery
of the Scarborough Tramways Company.

Published October 2007

ISBN 978 1 906008 15 4

© *Middleton Press, 2007*

Design Deborah Esher
Typesetting Barbara Mitchell

Published by
        Middleton Press
        Easebourne Lane
        Midhurst
        West Sussex
        GU29 9AZ
Tel: 01730 813169
Fax: 01730 812601
Email: info@middletonpress.co.uk
www.middletonpress.co.uk

Printed & bound by Biddles Ltd, Kings Lynn

CONTENTS

INTRODUCTION AND ACKNOWLEDGEMENTS

The ancient port and seaside resort of Scarborough was served by an electric tram system, worked by the Scarborough Tramways Company, which opened on 6th May 1904. The undertaking eventually operated 28 open-top cars running on a 3ft 6in/1067mm gauge over just under five miles of track which comprised two circular routes and three branches. Never really a successful enterprise, and operating only a restricted winter service, the tramway was acquired by the Corporation in 1931, on whose behalf United Automobile Services Ltd substituted motor buses after the closure of the system on 30th September of that year. The resort also boasted up to five cliff tramways, the earliest dating to 1875. Sadly, by 2007, only two of the lifts remained operative.

The bulk of the photographs illustrating this album come from the archives of the North Yorkshire County Council Library, Scarborough Museum and Gallery, the Scarborough Historical Society, and the Adam Gordon Collection; I am indebted to Jon Webster of the NYCCLIS, David Buchanan of Scarborough Museum, Colin Langford of the Scarborough Historical Society, Tony Carder and Norman Langridge have kindly read the proofs and Adam Gordon for their invaluable assistance in providing the pictures used. Other valuable images and information were kindly provided by Max Payne, Geoffrey Smith, Philip Battersby, Stanley King and Stephen Lockwood, to whom I also express my gratitude.

GEOGRAPHICAL SETTING

Scarborough is an ancient borough whose earliest inhabitants were Iron Age settlers occupying the promontory overlooking the North and South Bays. The Romans built a late 4th century signal station on the headland as an early warning system against Saxon pirates, whilst the Vikings established a stronghold in 966AD and gave the port its name of Skarthborg. The famous castle was built by William le Gros around 1130 during the reign of Henry I, and has endured several sieges during its long history. By the 19th century the town was a major East Coast shipbuilding centre, and its prominence as a spa was enhanced by the coming of the railways in the 1850s. It became a fashionable seaside venue during the late Victorian and Edwardian eras, and remains a popular resort, much visited during the summer months.

The town is situated at the southeast corner of the North York Moors, the Oolite of which forms substantial Limestone cliffs of varying height. The undulating landform gave an attractive area for residential development, the population rising to 38,000 by 1901.

HISTORICAL BACKGROUND

The Scarborough Tramway was owned and operated by the Scarborough Tramways Company, a subsidiary of Edmunson's Electricity Corporation Ltd, and opened on 6th May 1904. The route layout, on a 3ft 6in gauge, resembled a very rough figure eight laid on its side with Foreshore Road and Sandside on the South bay seafront to the east, Vernon Place at the central crossroads, and Scalby Road depot on the western edge. In addition a ¼ mile/402metres branch led northward from the western loop via Castle Road and North Marine Road past the cricket ground to the entrance to Alexandra Park, an area known as North Side or North Sands. A ¼ mile southern branch ran from the Aquarium along a private toll road to the Spa, mainly for concert traffic, whilst a link via Barwick Street and Hanover Road gave a shortcut across the western loop. The route mileage was 4.78/7.69km, of which roughly half was double track.

The service was originally worked by a fleet of 15 Brush-built open-toppers in a livery of dark red and cream. They were small vehicles, 26ft 6in/8.07metres long and 6ft 3in/1905mm wide, carrying 43 passengers and suited, like those of York and Chester, to the narrow back streets of the resort. They ran on Brush AA trucks of a short 5ft 6in/1676mm wheelbase, and were powered by two 35hp motors. They were soon joined by three British Electricity Car Company (BEC) trams (16-18) of a similar specification, but equipped for Raworth's Regenerative System. The following year Brush provided four more open-toppers (19-22), again with regenerative equipment, but running on Lycett-Conaty radial trucks which gave greater flexibility on curves. All the regenerative equipments are believed to have been removed between 1914-20.

A ¼ mile extension was opened eastwards from Sandside to a terminus (Marine Drive or South Sands) at the Marine Drive tollgate in 1906; this completed the system, which remained intact until receipts began to fall, mainly as a result of the World War. However, relations between Corporation and Company had never been good, largely as a result of problems with winter services (or lack of them). The latter insisted on restricting operations outside the summer season due to a shortage of passengers. As one of the motormen lucidly expressed it: 'no visitors – no service!' This policy remained a bone of contention over many years. After World War I some minor cutbacks to the network were implemented, though in 1925 the Company purchased six Brush tramcars (23-28) from Ipswich at a bargain price of £50 each. They boasted reversed stairs, and though longer than their stablemates, they were only 5ft 9in/1752mm wide. They carried 50 passengers and were mounted on 6ft/1828mm wheelbase Brush AA four-wheel trucks. Another car body was bought from Ipswich to replace Car 21, wrecked in an accident earlier that year. The body was fitted to the original truck and renumbered 21.

Scarborough also built and operated a number of cliff tramways. The first, known as the South Cliff Tramway, was also Britain's first ever cliff lift. It was opened on 6th July 1875, and like all its successors, operated on the funicular principle. Built to link the South Cliff with the Esplanade, it was 284ft/86.5metres long and is still running. The second lift was constructed to link the North Promenade Pier with Queen's Parade. It was the same length as the South Cliff lift and opened on 8th August 1878. Unfortunately the funicular was plagued with troubles during its short working life and a landslip effected its closure in 1887.

In 1881 a further cliff tramway was erected just north of the new Grand Hotel, designed to link the Foreshore with the town. The Central Tramway, which is 234ft/71.3metres long and opened on 1st August 1881 is still in operation under its original company. In 1929 another lift was built just south of the Grand Hotel on St Nicholas Cliff to ease pressure on passenger numbers using the Central Tramway. Opened on 5th August, the tramway ran the shortest distance of any, a mere 103ft/31.3metres. Sadly, it ceased operating in 2006 and looks much neglected. Finally in 1930, a tramway was established on the North Cliff, part of a large Corporation development of Peaseholm Gap. Opened in August of that year, the funicular was 165ft/50.2metres long. It ceased running in September 1996 and the components were removed, supposedly for reassembly at Launceston in Cornwall. Only two cliff lifts now remain in use, both in the South Bay, and it is a salutary fact that the oldest has now outlived the electric trams by 76 years.

In Parliament,
Session, 1902.

No. *1373*

29, Westborough,

Scarborough,

2nd December, 1901.

Scarborough Tramways.

Sir ~~or Madam~~,

We beg to inform you that application is intended to be made to Parliament in the ensuing Session for leave to bring in a Bill for an Act under the above name or short title, whereby it is proposed (amongst other things) to authorise the Promoters of the Undertaking to lay down a line of Tramway along *Falsgrave Road* and that in the part of that *Road* upon which the *Museum* ~~Numbered~~ in that *Road* of which we understand ~~you are~~ the *Scarborough Philosophical and Archæological Society are the Proprietors* abuts the Tramway will be laid as a *double* line and that a less space than nine feet six inches will intervene between the outside of the footpath on the *North East* side of the said *Road* and the nearest rail of the Tramway.

We are, Sir ~~or Madam~~,

Your obedient Servants,

TATE, COOK & FOWLER,

Solicitors for the Bill.

To *Sydney Previll Turnbull, Esqre*
Secretary
Scarborough Philosophical & Archæological Society,
St Thomas Street,
Scarborough.

P.S.—We beg to refer you to the annexed copies of the Standing Orders of the House of Lords and of the House of Commons which regulate the time and mode of presenting Petitions to those Houses respectively in opposition to Bills.

Standing Orders of the House of Lords—

32.—No Petition praying to be heard upon the merits against any Local Bill or Provisional Order Confirmation Bill originating in this House shall be received by this House, unless the same is presented by being deposited in the Private Bill Office before Three o'clock in the afternoon on or before the seventh day after the day on which such Bill has been read a second time.

93.—No Petition praying to be heard upon the merits against any Local Bill or any Provisional Order Confirmation Bill brought from the House of Commons shall be received by this House, unless the same be presented by being deposited in the Private Bill Office before Three o'clock in the afternoon on or before the seventh day after the day on which such Bill has been read a first time.

Standing Order of the House of Commons—

129.—No Petitioners against any Private Bill or any Bill to confirm any Provisional Order or Provisional Certificate shall be heard before the Committee on the Bill, unless their Petition shall have been prepared and signed in strict conformity with the Rules and Orders of this House, and shall have been presented to this House by having been deposited in the Private Bill Office, in the case of Private Bills, not later than Ten clear days after the first reading of such Bill, and in the case of Bills to confirm any Provisional Order or Provisional Certificate, not later than Seven clear days after notice shall have been given of the day on which the Bill will be examined, except where the Petitioners shall complain of any matter which may have arisen during the progress of the Bill before the said Committee, or of any proposed additional Provision, or of the Amendments as proposed in the filled-up Bill deposited in the Private Bill Office.

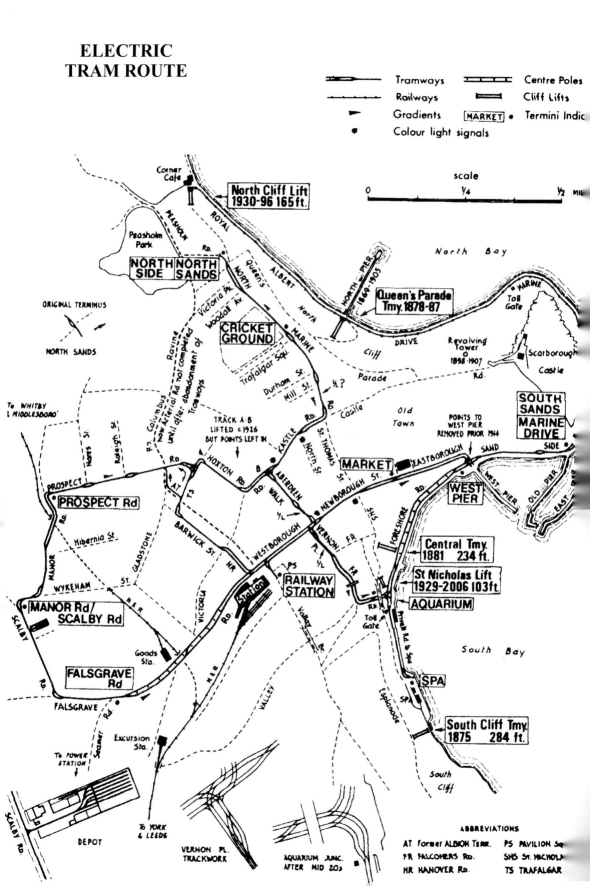

TRIALS

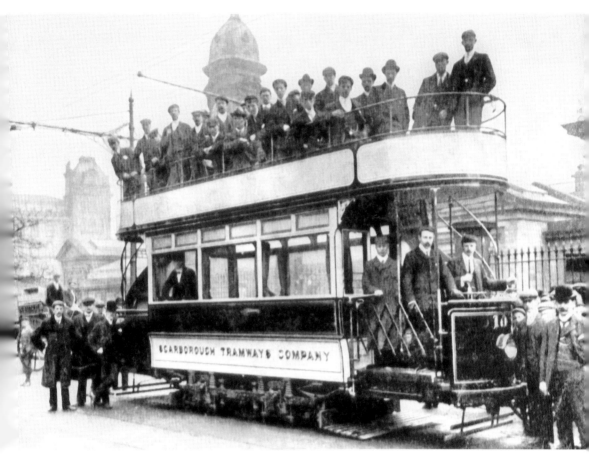

1. The Scarborough system consisted of a rough figure-of-eight layout with spurs leading off to the north, east and south. (A.V.Jinks)

2. Car 10 is on pre-service trials by the Central Railway Station, whose clock tower looms behind the tram. Some of the passengers are presumably Brush Company staff. Note the lack of destination boxes, and the lattice platform gates which were soon replaced by bars or chains.

OPENING DAY

3.   The tramway was officially opened on 6th May 1904 by the Mayoress, Mrs W. Morgan. This view shows cars 1 and 2, suitably bedizened, in the Scalby Road tramshed, in front of dense crowds, awaiting the turning on of the current.

4.   Car 1, driven by the manager, J.M. Edmunson, approaches the depot gates on the inaugural run. Thirteen of the fifteen trams, decorated in orange coloured drapings and evergreen garlands, took part in the parade.

5.   Car 1 with a veiled Mayoress Morgan on the platform, as the vehicle, bearing a shield depicting the Borough coat of arms, waits for the photographer. This tram was adorned with royal blue drapes and evergreens.

6.   Decorated cars 10 and 9 head down Westborough, with the Bar Congregational Church centre right, at the entrance to Aberdeen Walk. Note the high set roller blinds designating SPECIAL CAR.

7.	This view of car 3, in shadow, is further down the hill, whilst running along the single track down Newborough. The overhead wire at the centre right marks the turn into Aberdeen Walk.

8.	Another more lightly loaded decorated tram moves west towards the Central Station, in this shot taken above an interlace of overhead power and span wires. Details of the adornments show up well in this view, including the garlanded swags. The roadside carts are awaiting luggage from rail travellers.

AQUARIUM

9.   It is convenient to start the street-by-street survey of the tramway at the Aquarium - a series of glass roofed underground rooms devoted to amusement and constructed in the 1870s. This image shows the tracks being laid on heavy wooden sleepers placed over the main piers to protect the below-surface apartments which included a baths and ballroom. Some of the glazed roofing can be seen to the left, whilst the elegant Spa Bridge provides a useful vantage point for viewers. In the foreground are the "Jim Crows" for bending the rails.

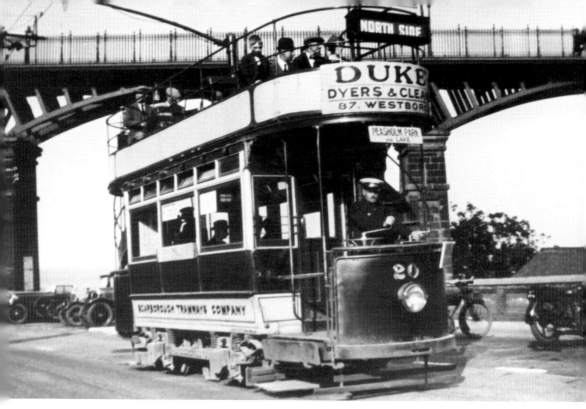

10.   Car 20 passes under the bridge in this 1929 scene, on its way to Peasholm Park in the North Bay.

11.   A tramcar passes the Rotunda Museum and the Aquarium on its way up the steep incline of Falconer's Road, seen on the left, which led into town via Vernon Place.

12.   Taken from the Spa Bridge, this shot shows a tram halted in much the same place as the previous picture. Falconer's Road is on the right, and the glass roofs of the Aquarium can be seen on both sides of the roadway. The elaborate roof, hung with bunting on the left covered the ballroom, into which an out of control car descended in 1925.

13.   Few, if any, images exist of trams on the spur leading to the Spa, but this photograph shows the tracks passing under the Spa Bridge and diverging on the left via a triangular junction onto the Foreshore at the bottom left, or along the roadway to the Spa complex. This latter thoroughfare featured a toll booth, as did the bridge.

14.   A fine panorama shows the appropriately named Grand Hotel, one of the largest in Europe when opened in 1870. The lady on the left seems somewhat overdressed for the weather! Above the Spa Cottage at the lower centre can be seen three trams on the Foreshore, whilst the line to the Spa can just be made out at the lower centre.

15.   A 1930 scene shows a car about to turn onto Foreshore Road. The set of tracks leading to the Spa can be seen at the bottom right, whilst the lines once forming the base of the triangular junction have long been lifted. The new St Nicholas Cliff Lift is on the left, above the entrance to Gala Land, the subterranean Aquarium.

FORESHORE ROAD

16.   A fine tramscape of the road, taken at the western end in 1904, shows the twin tracks and the elaborate scrolled and green-painted poles carrying the span wire supporting the overhead. The castle dominates the headland, whilst the latticed structure to the right of St Mary's Church on the skyline is the Warwick Revolving Tower, 155ft/47.2metres high, and affording superb views over both bays.

17.   Vast crowds swamp the beach and pavements as car 11 heads for Manor Road, passing alternative forms of transport visible on the left. The busy platform above the carriages was situated on St Nicholas gardens. Note the centre poles erected along this part of the route; their only other siting in Scarborough was along Falsgrave Road.

18.   Another tram, bearing an advert for the Aquarium, heads for the Marine Road terminus, whilst on the horizon can be seen the Old Pier and lighthouse.

19.   Car 24 halts by the Grand Pavilion, with its cinema, restaurant and skating rink. To the right of the tram are a line of East Yorkshire Motor Service single deck motorbuses. The film showing at the picture house, 'The Cradle Snatchers,' dates the image to 1927.

20.   Another busy scene shows two cars about to pass on the double track. Edwardians flocked to the resort in large numbers prior to World War I and in summer the South Beach was generally full.

21.　　A fine shot of a packed car 7 on the 6d (2.5p) Circular Tour gives a good view of the centre poles and twin tracks. The tower on the left belonged to the seawater swimming baths, later converted to a succession of different amusement purposes, and still standing today.

22.　　Stormy conditions prevail as car 13 battles the elements on its way round the bay. The presence of the Warwick Tower at the top left dates the picture to no later than 1907, when the structure was dismantled as an eyesore.

23.   Cars 21 and 12 approach each other along the Foreshore, with the tower of the seawater baths on the left, and horse carriages awaiting trade. Car 21 was totally wrecked in the 1925 Aquarium accident, and was rebuilt using a new body.

24.   Another tram pauses in front of what is now the 'Silver Dollar' arcade, an area that has changed out of all recognition since this Edwardian view was taken. Note the seafood stalls at the bottom right of the picture.

25.   Global warming was a concept alien to the Edwardians, but modern day visitors to Scarborough would doubtless blame it on the extreme weather conditions recorded here by the cameraman. The tramlines are completely submerged in this shot as an incredibly high winter tide swamps the whole seafront.

26.   Car 7 pauses by the West Pier bearing a PROSPECT ROAD sign above the dash panel with the fish sheds visible on the right - a 1920s image judging by the parked car seen on the left.

27.　　Car 2 is seen here at the stop opposite the West Pier, strangely bereft of adverts as the crew takes a few moments off for relaxation.

28.　　Car 24, ex-Ipswich, is with car 2 in another shot taken by the West Pier during the final summer of operations. Gala Land seems a popular attraction, plus the Fol-de-Rols who were appearing at the Floral Hall near the North Side terminus, the destination of car 24. Car 2 was operating the Circular route via Manor and Prospect Roads.

29.   Car 20 waits at the West Pier stop on its way to the South Sands terminus. Note the extra indicator boards above the roller blinds, amplifying the ones hung above the dash panel.

SANDSIDE

30.   A superb view of the entrance to Sandside, showing the twin rails narrowing to a single line on the left, and twin poles and span wire taking over from the centre posts. Car 19 can be seen alongside the Sandside Post Office, with the Wesleyan Chapel behind the tram pole. This panorama is full of interest, showing a fascinating cross section of Edwardians at play, with the castle walls towering above.

31.   Ex-Ipswich car 23, with its reversed stairs, is here parked at the South Sands/Marine Drive terminus, with its crew posing for the photographer.

32.   Taken from the south end of Marine Drive, opened in 1908, this scene shows a service car visible to the right of the lamp post at the same terminus. At this time the drive was a toll road, and the tollgate can be seen on the left, under the turreted gatehouse.

FALCONER ROAD

33.   Car 11 descends the steep slope of Falconer Road in this 1908 shot, about to take the curve left to the Aquarium. It is running the 3d Round-the-Town service, and the blind has not yet been adjusted from SCALBY ROAD.

34.   Car 9 grinds upwards round the curve into Falconer Road, with the Esplanade Hotel forming a backdrop, a sharp pull as the run up into town was the steepest on the system with a rise of one in ten/10% over 110ft/33.5metres. Car 21 went out of control and ran backwards at this point in 1925, ending up on the floor of the Aquarium ballroom.

VERNON PLACE

35.   Falconer   Road became Vernon Place at the top of the rise, and the tracklayers   designed   a complicated double loop near the junction with Westborough, embodying an interlaced line. This arrangement was laid to meet the requirements of   tradesmen   whose frontages needed delivery vehicles to be parked outside their premises throughout   the   day. Passing trams could use either line to circumvent these conveyances. The Domestic   Bazaar   on Westborough is now a branch of W.H. Smith.

36.   This view shows the tracks as laid, with a tram turning right into Westborough,   and   a second car following on behind. It is not known how much use was made of this complex layout.

CENTRAL RAILWAY STATION

37.   Car 10, on its way into town, passes the station in the early days of the enterprise. A further tram approaches in the distance. The Italianate design of the buildings included a massive clock tower. Note the almost complete absence of other traffic.

38.   Some 24 years later, and a much more animated scene greets the photographer, with motor cars, trams, buses and vans dominating the thoroughfare. The turreted building on the centre right is the Pavilion Hotel, built in 1870 and closed in 1971.

39.   Car 13 halts at the station stop on its way to Manor Road. The dashboard indicates both the Central and Excursion Stations as destinations, though the latter was some way off the tram route.

40.   Car 12 moves inbound in this late 1920s vista, as it passes the Victoria Hotel on the left, with the boundary wall of the station on the right. The overhead is here carried on a series of bracket poles.

WESTBOROUGH

41.   As its name implies Westborough forms part of a descending west-east roadway, which also includes Newborough and Eastborough, the last dropping steeply to join Foreshore Road. In this image car 5, bound for the North Side, halts on the spur line which ran right down Valley Bridge Road in front of the Pavilion Hotel.

42.   Car 2, on the Round-the-Town tour, pauses at the top of Westborough with the rails of the Hanover Road junction visible at the bottom left of the picture. The motorman is about to use his point iron for the vehicle to proceed straight ahead. The presence of primitive looking motor vehicles suggests an early 'twenties date for the picture.

43.   Taken just below the previous photograph, car 16, on its way to Scalby Road, leads an elegant looking horse drawn carriage. The North Eastern Hotel stands on the left in front of the cyclist, whilst the high set indicator boxes on the tram show an early date for the shot.

44.   Further down Westborough the lines forming the triangular junction with Vernon Place on the right can be seen curving into the roadway as car 9 grinds up this pleasant incline whose young trees suggest a future leafy thoroughfare. On this stretch of the undertaking the overhead wires are carried on decorated twin poles.

45.   Car 10 passes the Londesborough Theatre on the right in 1905 on its way uphill. The theatre became a cinema in 1914 and was demolished in 1959. The turreted edifice at the top left is Rowntrees Department Store, built in the French Renaissance style and opened in 1882.

⟶ 46.   Car 5 halts outside Rowntrees Store en route to Prospect Road, a view which picks out the elegant lines of the building. On the left two liveried top-hatted gents drive a horse carriage downhill in this early 20th century tramscape.

⟶ 47.   This image of tracklaying along Westborough shows clearly the disruption such major road engineering caused. A set of lines snake out of Vernon Place on the right and disappear into Aberdeen Walk on the left, whilst the main double track merges into one at the entrance to Newborough. This length of single line ran for only 500ft/152metres before doubling again, an inexplicable feature, as lights had to be erected to control the trams at this point.

48.   A tram proceeds uphill with the Rowntree building standing just right of the centre of the picture. At the extreme right is the Bar Congregational Church, whilst in front of the car the spur lines turn right into Aberdeen Walk. Vernon Place is on the left, with the rails turning into it just visible under the wheels of the nearest carriage.

A	7693	
THE SCARBOROUGH		
TRAMWAYS COMPANY.		
UP	Aquarium	3D
	West Pier	
	Vernon Place	CIRCULAR TICKET
	Railway Station	
	Raleigh Street	
	Depot	
	Seamer Road	DOWN
	Issued subject to the bye-laws.	

49.　　In this 1930 shot, car 5 halts just before Vernon Place on the right, whose tracks can be seen in the roadway. The policeman is directing traffic coming out of Aberdeen Walk, whilst the double deck motor bus is obviously a sign of things to come.

ZL 4465

Up	Scalby Road	S. T. Co. 2d Not Transferable Down
	Vernon Place	
	Floral Hall	
	Raleigh Street	
	Aquarium	
	Seamer Road	
	Castle Road	
	Londesboro' Road	
	South Toll House	
	Market	
	Spa	
	Colmb. Bay. P.O.	
	West Pier	
	Railway Station	
	Aberdeen Walk	
	School of Art	
	North Bungalows	

Tickets available for punched Section. To be shown on demand.

Bell Punch Co., Uxbridge.

NEWBOROUGH

50.   The short stretch of single track can be seen heading down Newborough, whilst the descending tramcar is bound for the West Pier. In this busy scene, full of interest, bracket poles have taken over from the twin posts and span wire, common to Westborough. Note Boots the Chemists on the right, with its fashionable clock.

51.   Another view looking down the steep route shows the single line and bracket poles running down the right hand side of this busy street.

52.   St Nicholas Street on the right, with Boots on the corner, marked the reversion to double track, with the bracket poles shifting to the other side of the roadway. This engaging scene features elegant Edwardian ladies, whilst the policeman at the bottom right is wearing the peculiar light coloured helmet seen on other Scarborough 'Bobbies.' A distinctive row of lamps runs along the top of the chemist's plate glass windows.

53.   The eastern end of Newborough continues downhill towards Eastborough with the tram tracks remaining double, and the overhead wires suspended on side poles.

EASTBOROUGH

54.   This picture looks uphill with Eastborough commencing at St Helen's Square which leads off at the top right. Contemporary photographs show plenty of horse drawn transport interspersed among the tramlines, which must have made the upward pull hard for the beasts.

55.   The lower end of the hill has Post Street leading off on the left, and shows the tram tracks lined with stone setts. The sandbagged barricade dates from 1915, one of several breaching the rails, and was erected when there were fears of a German invasion.

56.   This thoroughfare was the only one apart from the Foreshore to boast centre poles, though these were replaced in the 1920s in the face of increased traffic density. In this view, car 14 is taking passengers on the 3d Round-the-Town trip - a half price version of the 6d run.

57.   Two trams, including car 4, pose side-by-side along the tree lined highway, another early image with the crews wearing distinctly non-regulation headgear!

58.   Car 16 is pictured along the same road bearing its riders along the 6d Circular Route. This tour gave passengers more than five miles of travel and was very popular in fine weather.

59.   Car 3 passes a creeper clad All Saint's Church on its way into town, an image which shows the boulevard like nature of the street with its lines of growing trees. The church has now been replaced with a block of shops and flats.

60.   The western end of Falsgrave Road saw the double line revert to single track, with Seamer Road heading off to the right of the photograph.

SCALBY ROAD

61.   This shot was taken on the loop joining Falsgrave and Scalby Roads. The occasion is unknown, though the police officer was evidently deemed necessary to keep order! Both trams, including car 8, are heading for the station, and each platform carries a splendidly behatted lady.

TRAM DEPOT

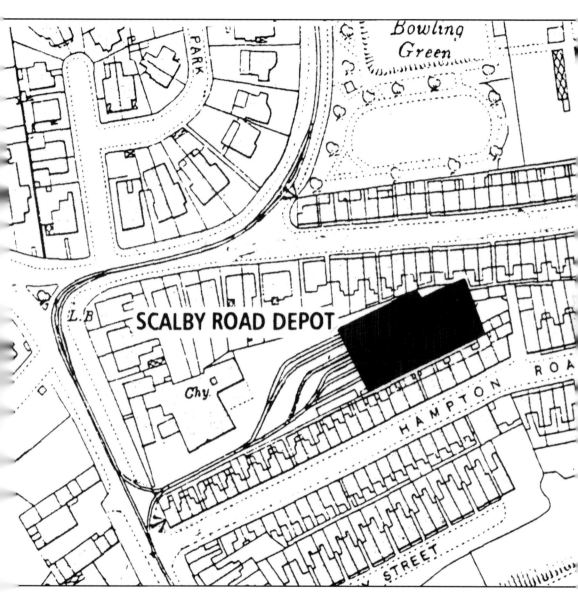

62.   The tramshed was situated on Scalby Road and the plan shows how it was squeezed in between blocks of terraced houses. Six tracks led out from the depot, eventually contracting into one, with a triangular junction allowing cars to turn both ways into Scalby Road.

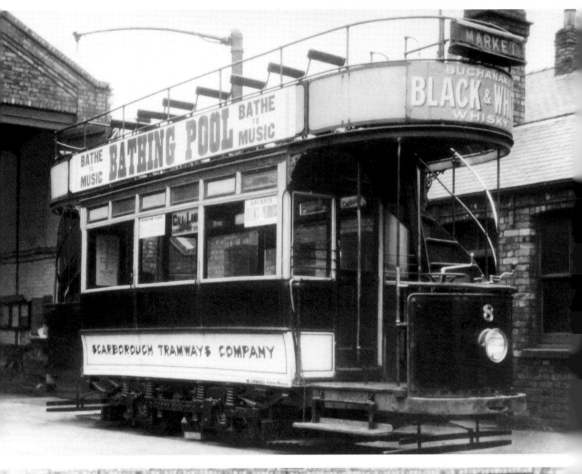

←———— 63. A good study of car 8 was taken in 1929 in the depot yard; its roller blind shows MARKET as its destination. Note the curvature of the tram body, a product of hard riding on the 25 year old vehicle.

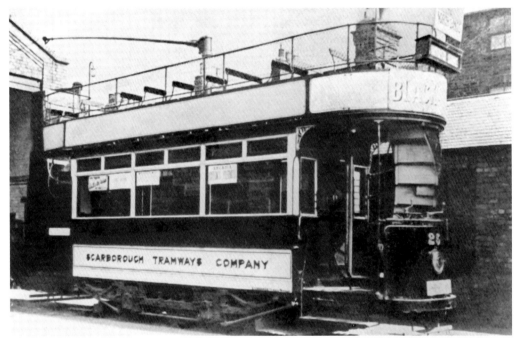

←———— 64. Cars 3, 22 and 12, stand outside the shed, occupying three of the six tracks. Car 3 is bound for the Floral Hall. Car 22 is plying between the North and South Bays, whilst 12 is running via the Central Station.

65. Ex-Ipswich car 25, identified by its reversed stairs, is in the yard and carries fewer adverts than most of its stablemates.

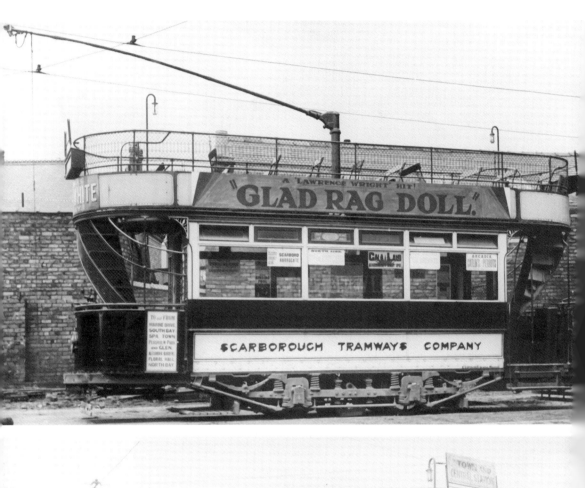

66.　　An absorbing shot of car 26, gives a good view of its 6ft Brush AA truck. The tram displays a wealth of adverts, including examples promoting a cricket match, Gala Land, Catlin's Pierrots at the Arcadia, and a North Side Circus. Inside is a bill indicating that the Futurist is screening Al Jolson's 'Singing Fool,' the first 'talkie' released in 1929.

67.　　Another engaging picture of the depot yard, evidently taken at the same time as 63, shows cars 25, 21 and 8. Car 21 was reconstructed from the vehicle wrecked in the Aquarium crash of 1925. It was fitted with an Ipswich body and the original radial truck. Note the extra destination boards above the roller blinds on this vehicle, and the young lady coyly posing on the left.

68.　　The demolition of the tramshed in the 1990s shows that the tramlines still remained in the depot floor, with the inspection pits clearly visible underneath.

MANOR ROAD

69.　　Local photographers rarely ventured into the terraced back streets of the resort, so that views of trams in these areas are largely non-existent. This image, taken on the turnout joining Scalby Road with Manor Road, shows car 3 at the stop, whilst a sea cadet band proceeds noisily towards Wykeham Street. The open ground to the right of the tram contained a nursery and bowling green.

70.   Photographically a neglected part of the undertaking, this view shows car 2 pausing in front of the terraced housing lining this thoroughfare. Note the board below the centre window showing that the route traverses Prospect and Falsgrave Roads.

CASTLE ROAD

71.   One of a number of triangular junctions featured along the tramway, this example joins Castle Road on the left with Aberdeen Walk on the right. Though doubled at the junction, both streets were single line along their length. Here both highways are completely blocked by tracklaying operations.

72.   This narrow street carried a single line with one passing loop, which a tram is just about to enter on its way north-west, with the General Post Office on the left. A cyclist weaving to avoid the rails has managed to obscure the fleet number of the car in the process!

NORTH MARINE ROAD

73.   This route ran as single line with turnouts alongside the North Bay as far as Alexandra Gardens and the Floral Hall which was opened in 1910 and demolished in 1988. In this view one of the tramcars nears the loop by Albert Street, with Dent's Family Grocers (now Wray's newsagents) on the left.

74. Further north, car 16 halts on the Trafalgar Square turnout just above the cricket ground, famous for its September Festivals. It is evidently washday, judging by the lines hung out in front of the terraces on the right. On this part of the system the running wire was carried on bracket poles.

75. Ex-Ipswich 24 halts near the terminal loop as passengers disembark to partake of the pleasures of the North Bay, including Peasholm Park and the sands.

SCARBOROUGH TRAMWAYS COMPANY

76.   An ex-Ipswich tram waits on the turnout for trade into town in this 1929 scene, with the Floral Hall on the left and Clarence Gardens Hotel (now the Boston Hotel) to the right.

77.   Two fairly crowded cars stand side-by-side on the same loop. Where the group in front of the trams is heading is uncertain, but the equestrian gentlemen are obviously not awaiting a ride on either tram!

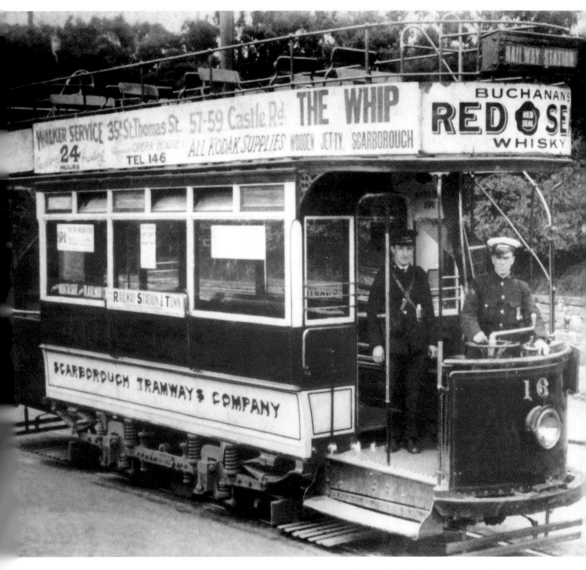

78.   Car 16, with roller blind and side board reading RAILWAY STATION is posed at the North Side terminus together with its crew. A variety of adverts adorn its upper deck decency board, so called because it prevented female ankles being seen.

79. Car 21 is here pictured at the same spot and heading in the same direction in this 1926 image, taken after the vehicle had been rebuilt following its descent into the Aquarium ballroom the previous year. In contrast with car 16 it is totally bereft of exterior advertising.

AQUARIUM ACCIDENT

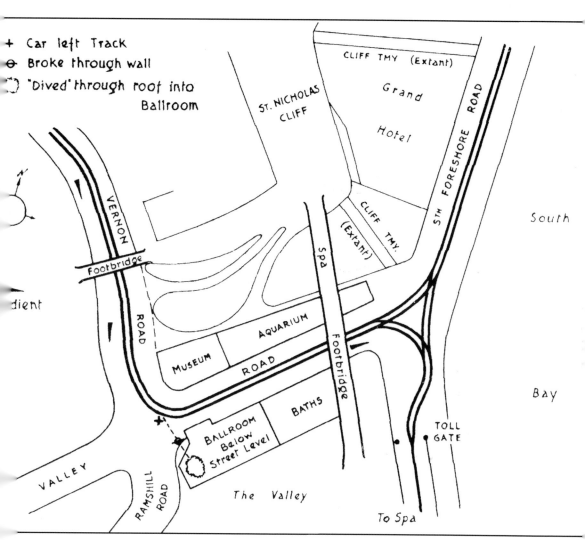

+ Car left Track
⊖ Broke through wall
⊃ 'Dived' through roof into Ballroom

CLIFF TMY (Extant)

Grand
Hotel

ST. NICHOLAS CLIFF

STH FORESHORE ROAD

South

CLIFF TMY. (Extant)

N

VERNON ROAD

Footbridge

Spa

dient

AQUARIUM ROAD

Footbridge

MUSEUM

BATHS

Bay

BALLROOM Below Street Level

TOLL GATE

VALLEY

RAMSHILL ROAD

The Valley

To Spa

80.   On 16th September 1925, car 21 skidded on greasy rails and experienced brake failure whilst climbing Falconer Road (now Vernon Road). It ran backwards, gathering speed, left the track, demolished the retaining wall and crashed through the glass roof of the subterranean Aquarium ballroom. This plan shows the layout of the area and the place where the car jumped the rails. (*Tramway Review*/H.V. Jinks).

81. In the foreground of this postcard can be seen the grooves cut in the road by the tram wheels, and the hole in the glass roof of the ballroom. Part of the upper deck of the car remains hanging, suspended from the roof girders.

82. The eight ton vehicle fell some thirty feet into the ballroom, mercifully avoiding the caretaker who had just finished sweeping the floor! The conductor, Harry Wyke and the few passengers baled out before the impact, but the gallant motorman George Smith stayed with his charge and was rescued, dazed but unharmed. When brought round, he seemed to think he had been under bombardment in the World War I trenches!

⟶ 83. Another view of the wrecked car, which was garlanded with bunting torn from the ballroom ceiling. Though the top deck was stripped clear of seats and rails, most of the tram windows remained unbroken!

FINAL DAY

84.   A busy scene on Westborough with Valley Bridge Road at the bottom right, as three trams, including ex-Ipswich 27, help to provide a service on the last day of operations, 30th September 1931. Note the mini roundabout, and the charabanc plying the route to Oliver's Mount. The demolition at centre left was connected with the construction of a new road, Northway, through the town centre.

85.   A close up of car 27 shows well the arrangement of its upper deck seating and reversed stairs, the latter a nuisance to motormen trying to see to their left. The vehicle does not seem overly thronged with riders giving it a last farewell.

DECORATED TRAMS

86. The resort had a fine tradition of embellishing their vehicles for special occasions. In November 1914 the depot staff produced this splendid 'Armoured Tram' to help with recruitment to the armed forces. 'John Willie' was a fictitious northern music hall character, sung of by George Formby senior and other comedians. Less than a month after this car appeared two German battlecruisers emerged from the morning mists and subjected Scarborough to a heavy bombardment, a war crime which led to the rallying cry 'Remember Scarborough!'

⟶ 87. In March 1918 the town organised a 'Submarine Week' to raise £100,000 for the purchase of an underwater vessel for the Royal Navy. In pursuit of this objective the undertaking constructed this singular reproduction, complete with conning tower and torpedo tubes, here seen on the spur outside the Pavilion Hotel.

88.   Equally noteworthy was this ambitious design on a 'Feed the Guns' motif, which was aired in November in the very week the war ended. This outstanding example of innovative design bore the watchwords of national significance.

89.   At the end of the war car 11 was embellished with garlands and flags to commemorate the cessation of hostilities. It is here shown posed for the camera in November 1918.

90.   Not the finest example of a decorated Scarborough tram, this crowded vehicle, halted under the Spa Bridge, was run in aid of the Mission to Seamen, some of whom appear on the upper deck of the car.

91.   In 1920 this tram, seen here on the Foreshore, was decked out to encourage funding for the war memorial to honour Scarborough's dead. The monument, a tall obelisk, was subsequently erected on Oliver's Mount.

92.   This vehicle, with its many flags and bunting, seems to have been adorned to attract visitors to the resort. Note the 6d Round-the-Town board on the dash, and the distinctly non-standard lettering on the rocker panel.

93.   Nicely dated on the rocker panel, Car 11 is here on display outside the Westboro' Hotel for the 1921 Charity Carnival. Another triumph for the depot staff, the tram actually won first prize! The board above the motorman wishes success to the extension of the holiday season, whilst another on the dash panel indicates that the tram is plying between the West Pier and Seamer Road.

———→ 94.   A great success was this superb 1929 tribute to the Festival Cricketers and here on show in the depot yard. Car 8 is being driven by Chief Inspector Gubbins with the tramway mascot 'Spot' posed in front.

95.   An equally charming photograph shows depot staff on and around the car, including the chief clerk, Alfred Leadbeater, seen on the right. 'Spot' is accompanied on the platform step by the pet cat, though how they were made to stay still for the camera remains a mystery!

96.   Another distinctive decorated car was this example, dressed up for the local hospital bazaar and seen here preparing for its inaugural run, again in the depot yard.

97.   This tramcar was an illuminated example, and is displayed here in lit-up mode. It must have been a fine sight as it proceeded along the system in the dark.

CARS AND CREWS

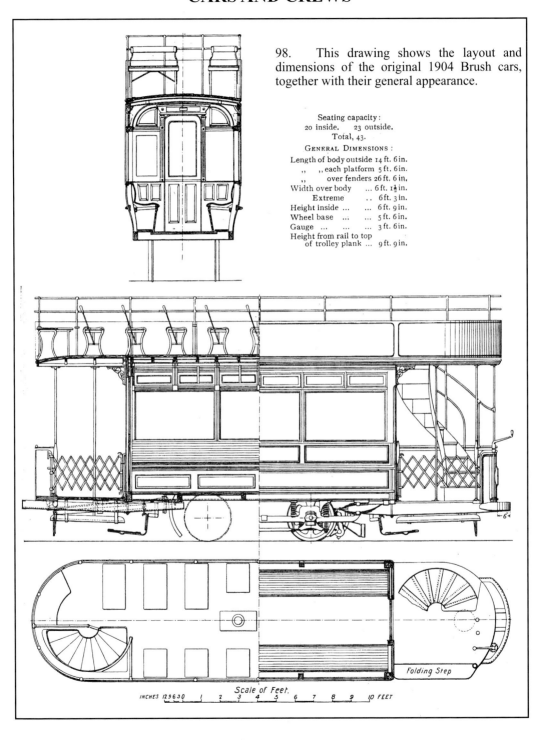

98.   This drawing shows the layout and dimensions of the original 1904 Brush cars, together with their general appearance.

Seating capacity:
20 inside.   23 outside.
Total, 43.

GENERAL DIMENSIONS :

Length of body outside 14 ft. 6 in.
,,   ,, each platform 5 ft. 6 in.
,,   over fenders 26 ft. 6 in.
Width over body   ... 6 ft. 1½ in.
        Extreme   .. 6 ft. 3 in.
Height inside ...   ... 6 ft. 9 in.
Wheel base   ...   ... 5 ft. 6 in.
Gauge   ...   . 3 ft. 6 in.
Height from rail to top
    of trolley plank ... 9 ft. 9 in.

Folding Step

Scale of Feet.
INCHES 129630   1   2   3   4   5   6   7   8   9   10 FEET

99.   Car 5 appears in pristine condition on delivery in its livery of dark red and cream. It boasts interior curtains, and the high set indicator boards were soon lowered to just below the top of the front rails.

100.   The cosy interior of the same tram shows the polished wooden longitudinal seating, curtains, lamps in pear shaped globes and the looped straps for standing passengers.

101.   An early shot of car 8, already bedecked with adverts, again shows the high set indicator boxes. Although the motorman is in uniform, the conductor appears in 'civvies.' The latter is holding on to one of the soon-to-be discarded lattice platform gates.

——→ 102.   Tramcars were often hired out for functions, and this excellent study shows car 15 doing duty as a wedding carriage. Toppers and fancy hats abound. The happy couple can be seen at the lower left of the image. The top deck is fully crowded with equally well turned out wedding guests in this delightful photograph.

——→ 103.   Tramway undertakings often embodied sporting and social clubs, and Scarborough was no exception. This 1914 picture shows the staff football team in front of one of the cars, which is advertising a charity football match versus the electricity supply eleven on the South Sands. Judging from the look of the team, the opposition need have no reason to tremble!

104.   Chief Inspector Gubbins, resplendent in his official uniform, poses for his photograph near the tramway offices on Scalby Road.

105.   At the closure of the tramway, chief clerk Alfred Leadbeater takes a last look at the premises in this scene taken in the depot yard.

CLIFF LIFTS

106.   This view shows the earliest of the lifts, on the South Cliff, here shown in Edwardian times before the lower station was obscured by later buildings. The funicular rose 284ft from the beach to the Esplanade.

107.   This scene shows the two cars passing on the steep trackway. Built in 1875 the tramway
has at various times been powered by water, gas, and latterly electricity.

108.   The lift was closed for refurbishment in early 2007 and this shot pictures the cars halted halfway up the incline whilst repairs were being made.

109.   The same cars seen from the Esplanade station, showing the steep one in two/50% incline of the tramway.

110. A rare and perhaps unique view depicts the North Cliff tramway, constructed in 1878 to link the Promenade Pier with Queen's Parade. The top station and one of the cars show up clearly in the picture. The funicular was plagued with problems and was dismantled after a landslip after only nine years of working.

111. The Central Lift was built in 1881 to link the Foreshore with the town. Rising 234ft, it was opened in 1881 and is one of only two cliff tramways still operating in Scarborough.

112.   This 1950s image shows one of the cars at the upper station, the most elaborate of all the cliff lift buildings.

113.   This 2007 shot provides a good view of the gradient of this tramway, with its slope of one-in-two.

114.   One of the Central Tramway cars is seen here at the upper station awaiting passengers for the downward run.

⟶ 115. In 1929 the St Nicholas lift was built to ease pressure on the Central Tramway which lies on the opposite side of the Grand Hotel, seen here above the lift. The ride is only 103ft long, and this photograph was taken shortly after it was opened. The electric tramlines are still in place in the road below, and the entrance to the underground Gala Land can be seen at the foot of the funicular.

116.   A later image shows the lift in operation, ——————➤ 117.   A 1967 photograph of one of
carrying riders from the beach to town. The   the St Nicholas cars and the top station also reveals
short length of the trip can be appreciated in   the South Beach and castle. These cars were later
this shot.   replaced with more up to date vehicles.

——————➤ 118.   The two St Nicholas cars stand forlorn halfway up the slope after the closure of
the tramway in 2006.

119.   The last of the Scarborough lifts to be built was on the North Cliff, part of a scheme to develop the Peasholm Gap. Opened in 1930, the tramway was 165ft long. Both stations can be seen in this 1960s image.

120.   The lift is seen here in its 1930s heyday, operating at the busy Corner Café area, and taking riders up to Peasholm Road. Declining passenger numbers forced its closure in 1996 and it was dismantled subsequently.

MIDDLETON PRESS

EVOLVING THE ULTIMATE RAIL ENCYCLOPEDIA

Easebourne Lane, Midhurst, West Sussex.
GU29 9AZ   Tel:01730 813169
www.middletonpress.co.uk   email:info@middletonpress.co.uk
A-978 0 906520 B- 978 1 873793 C- 978 1 901706 D-978 1 904474 E - 978 1 906008

OOP Out of print at time of printing - Please check availability   BROCHURE AVAILABLE SHOWING NEW TITLES